PAISLEY

DESIGNS WITH A SPLASH OF COLOR

Marty Noble

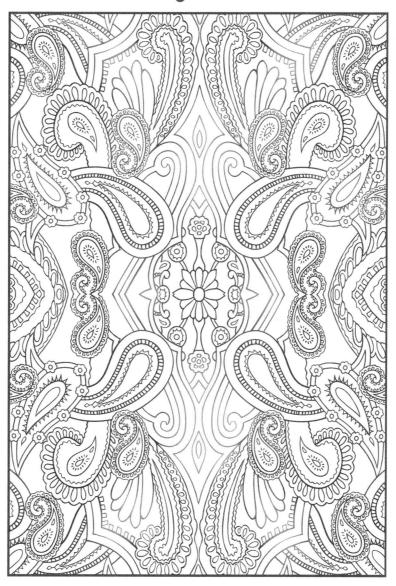

DOVER PUBLICATIONS, INC.
MINEOLA, NEW YORK

For centuries, artists and artisans have been captivated by the hypnotic appeal of paisley designs. Each of these thirty-one twisted tear-drop patterns is printed in a variety of brilliant hues that add extra verve to the coloring experience. Pages are perforated and printed on one side only for easy removal and display. *Paisley: Designs with a Splash of Color* and other *Creative Haven* coloring books offer an escape to a world of inspiration and artistic fulfillment.

Bibliographical Note
Paisley: Designs with a Splash of Color, first published by Dover Publications, Inc., in 2016, is a republication with color of *Paisley Designs Coloring Book,* originally published by Dover in 2008.

International Standard Book Number
ISBN-13: 978-0-486-80776-8
ISBN-10: 0-486-80776-2

Manufactured in the United States by RR Donnelley
80776201   2016
www.doverpublications.com

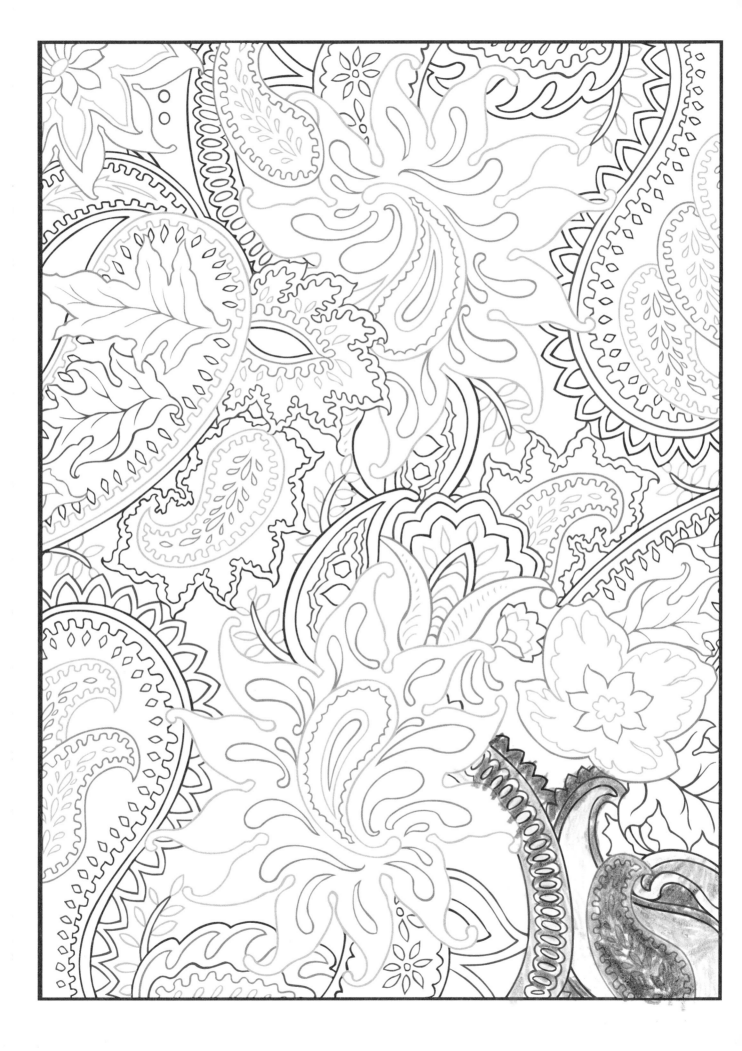

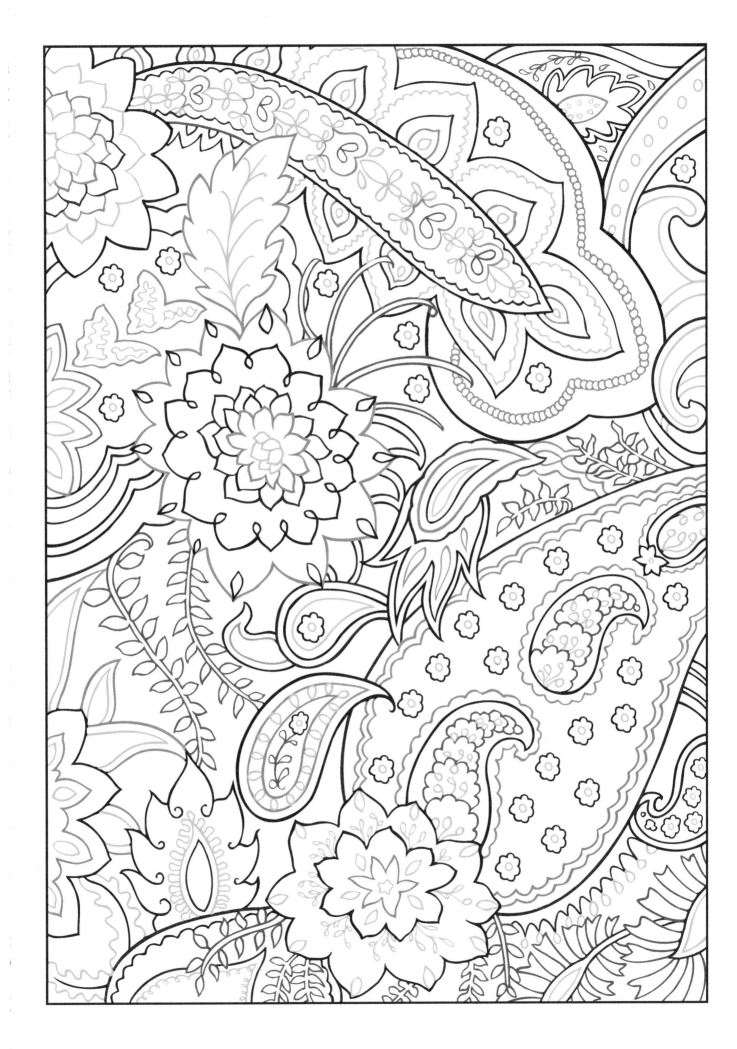

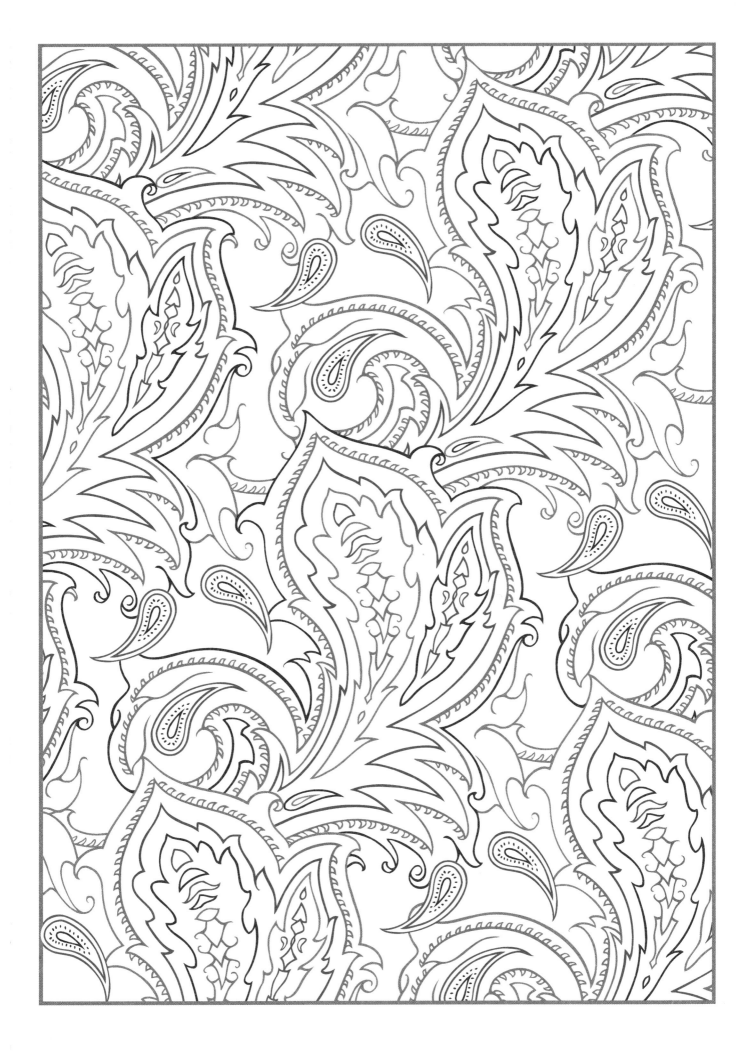

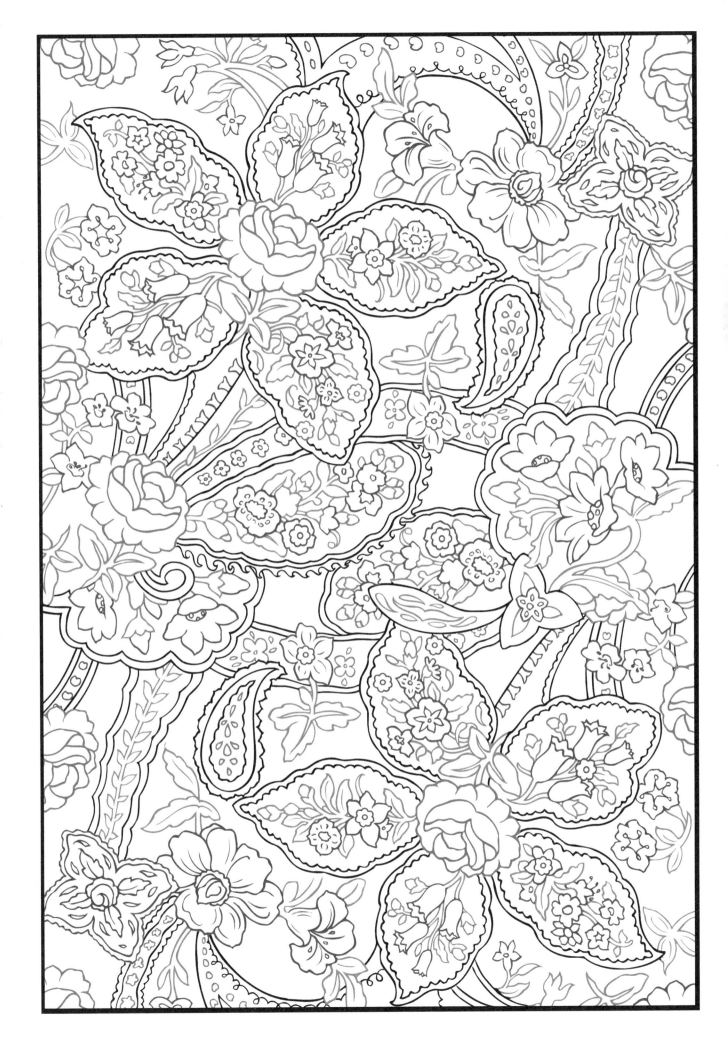

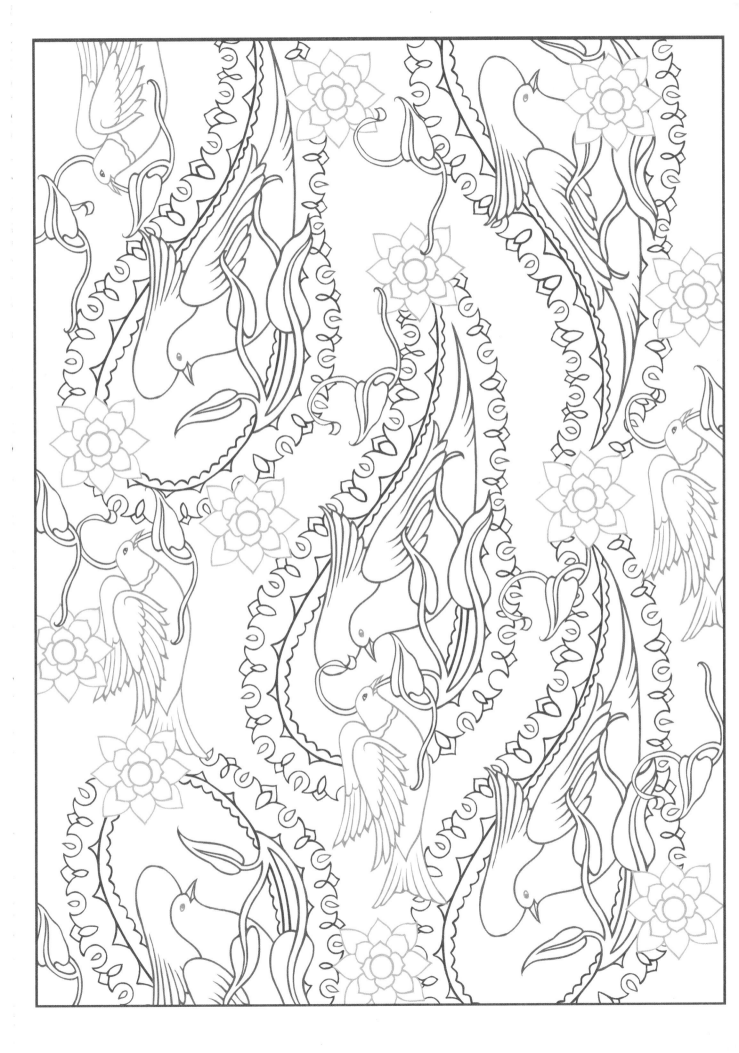

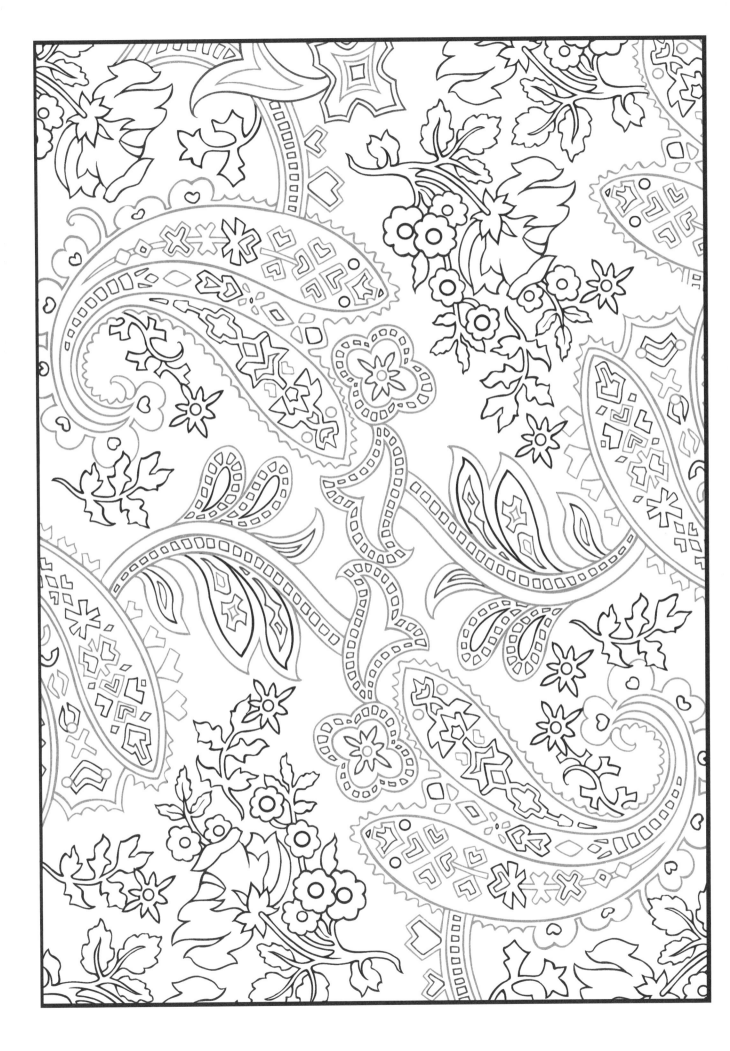

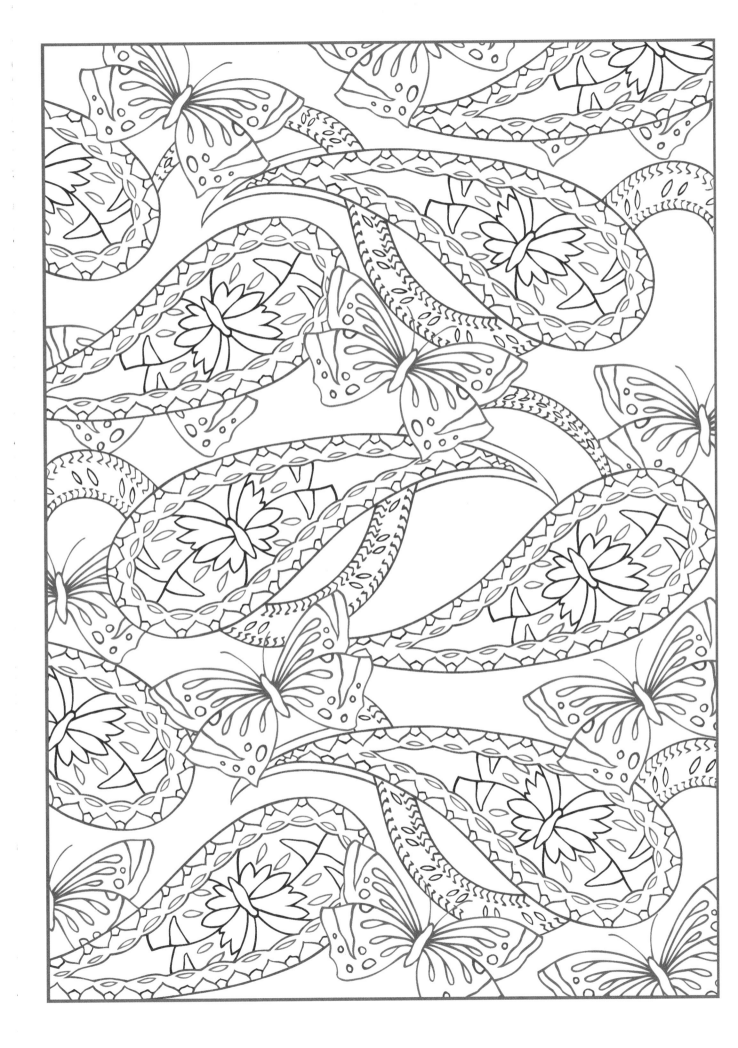

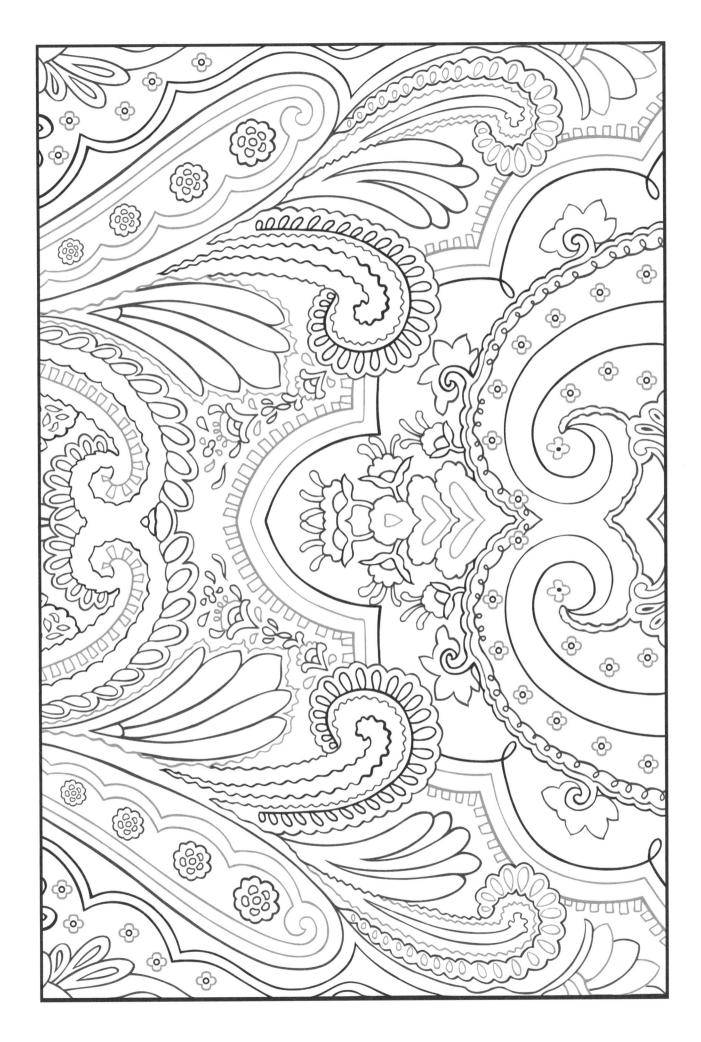

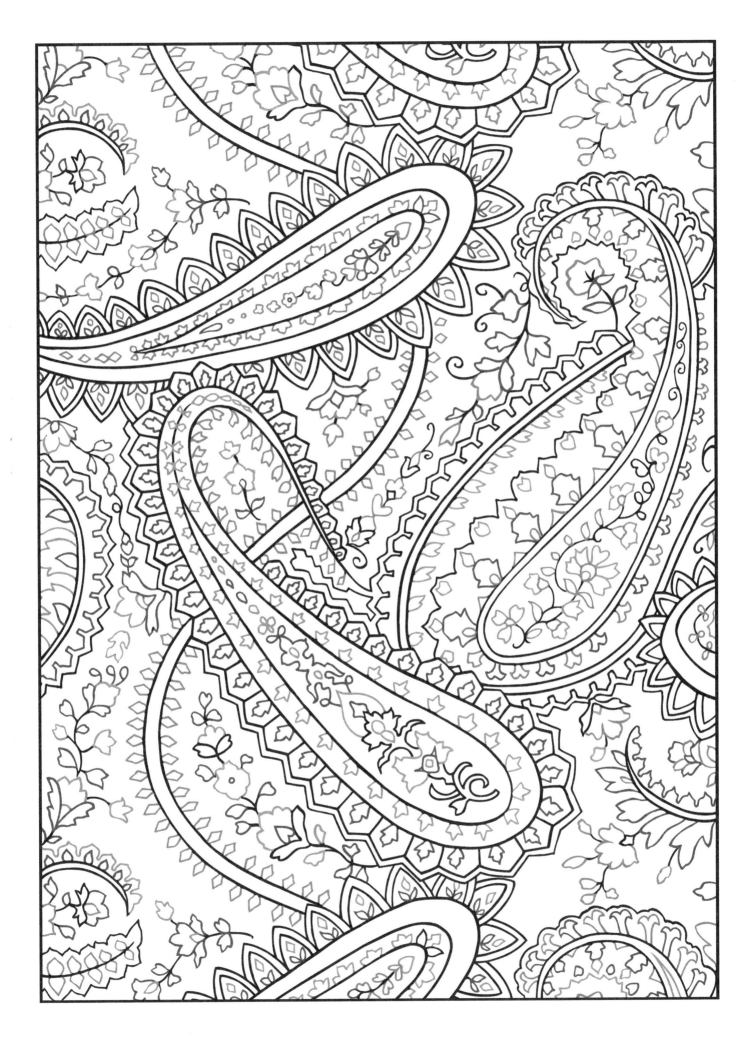

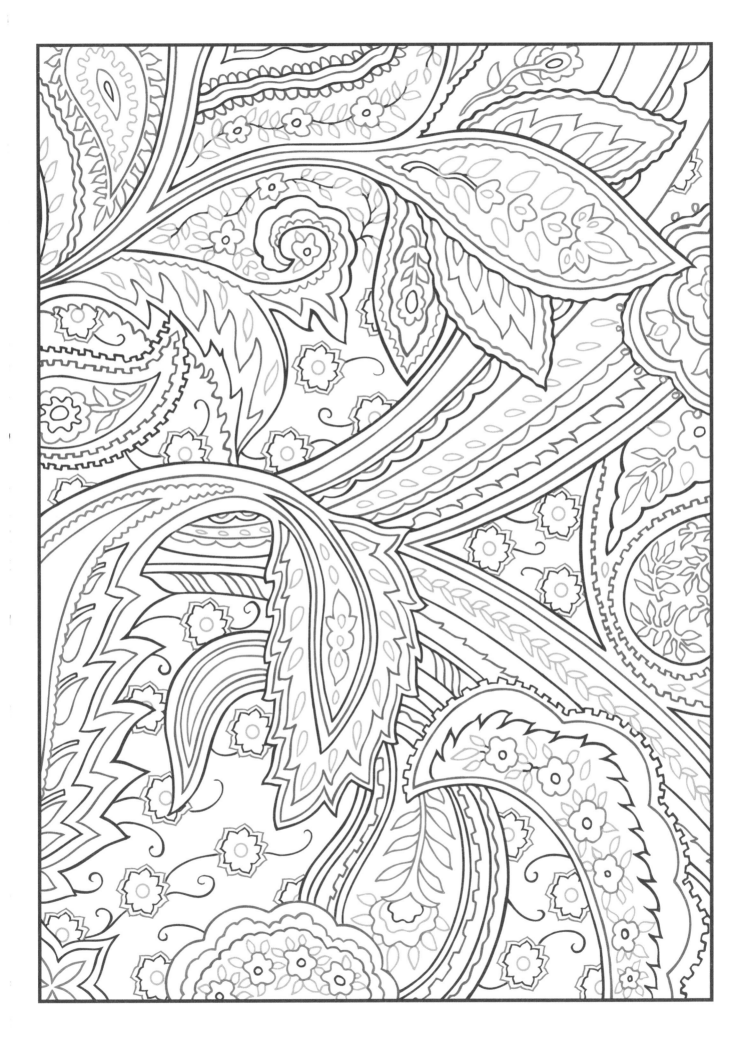

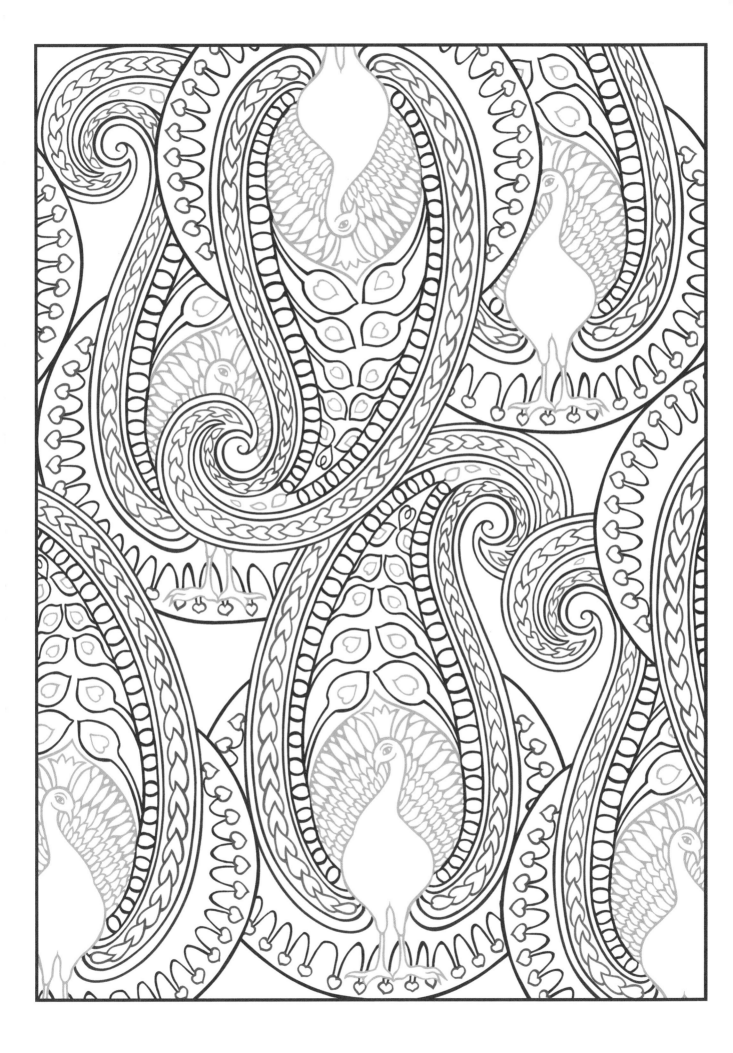

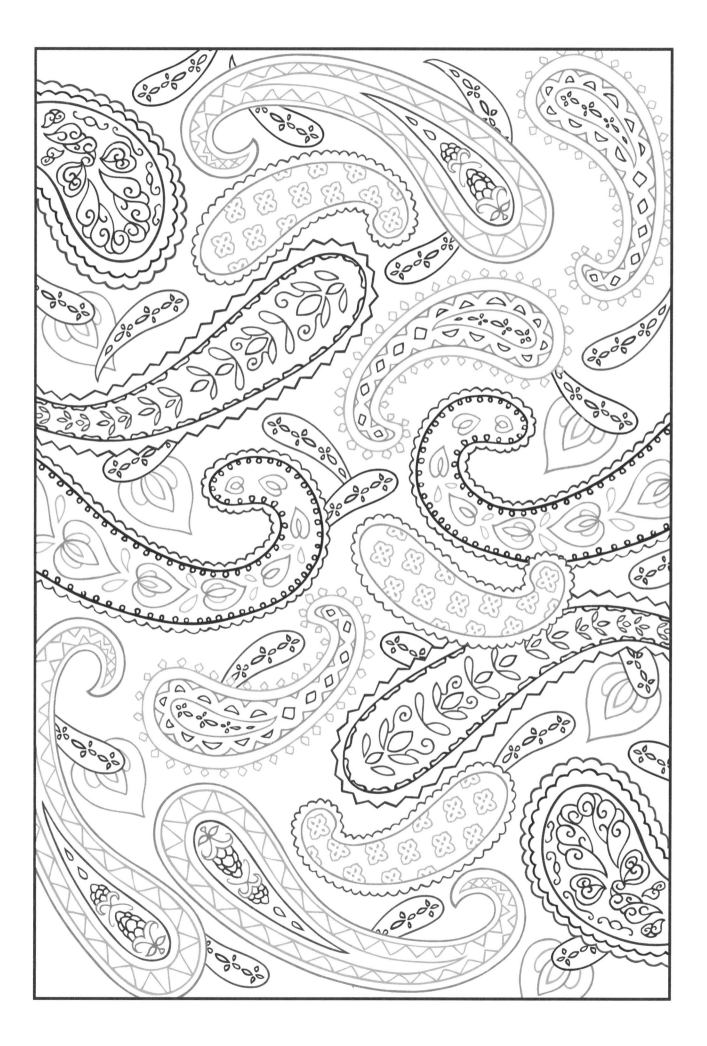

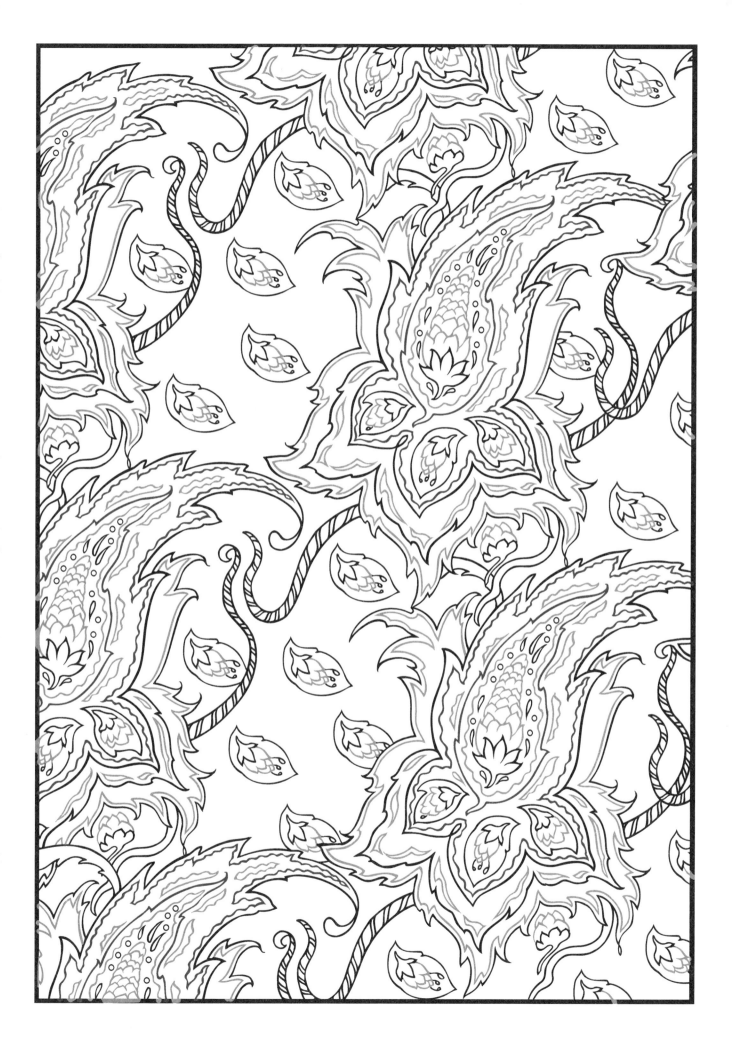

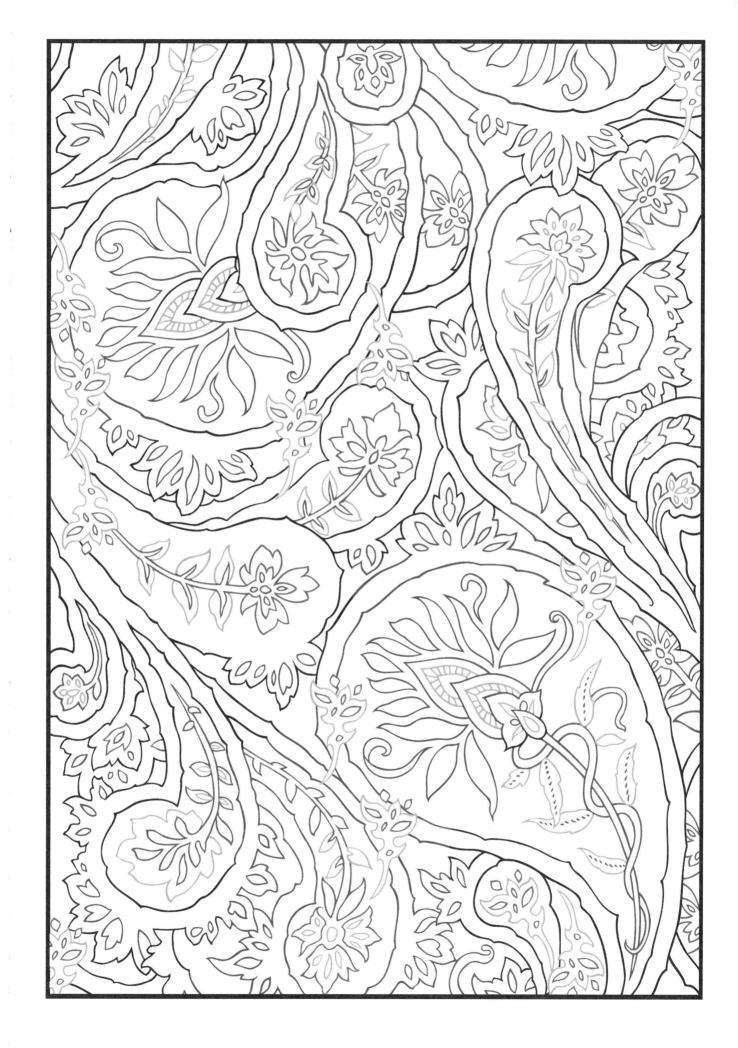

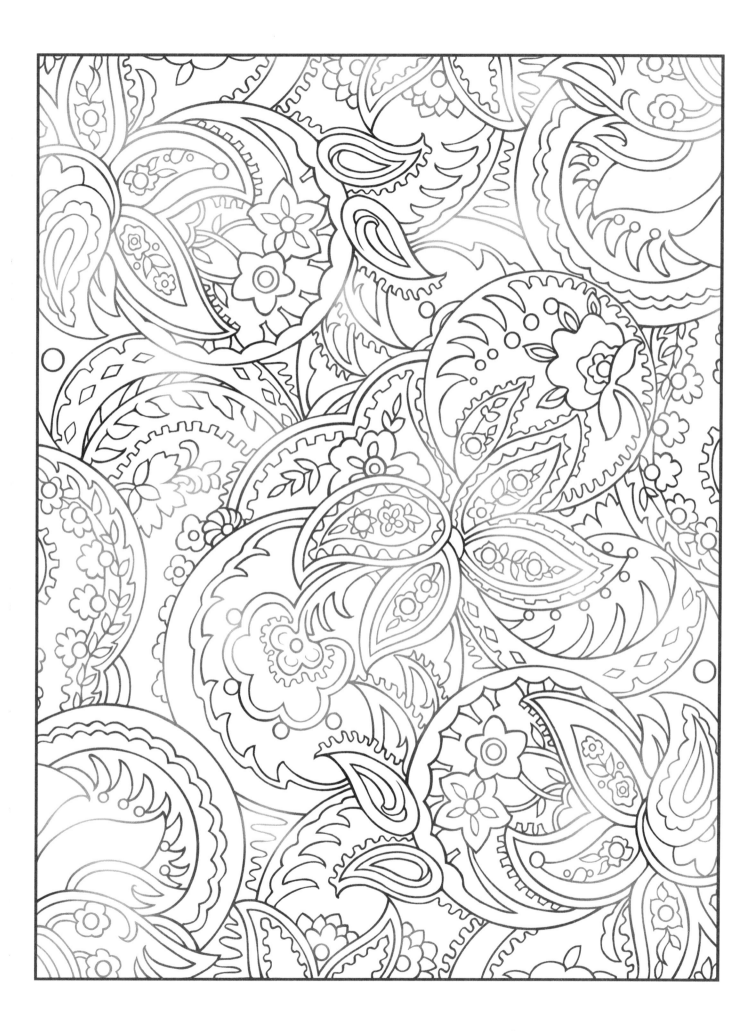

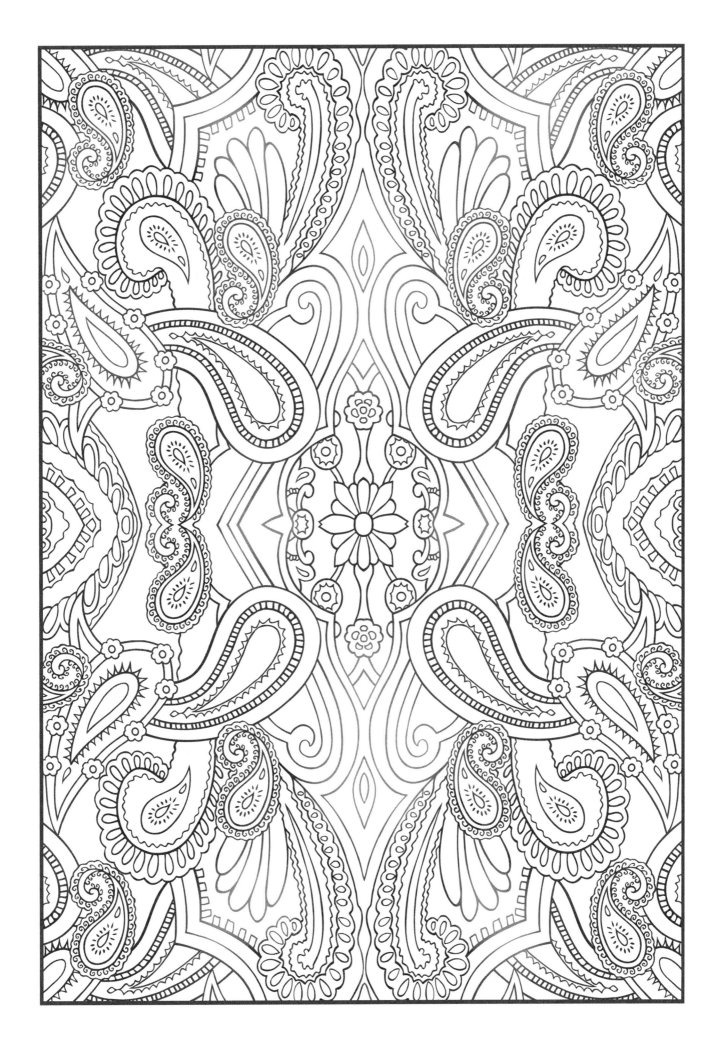

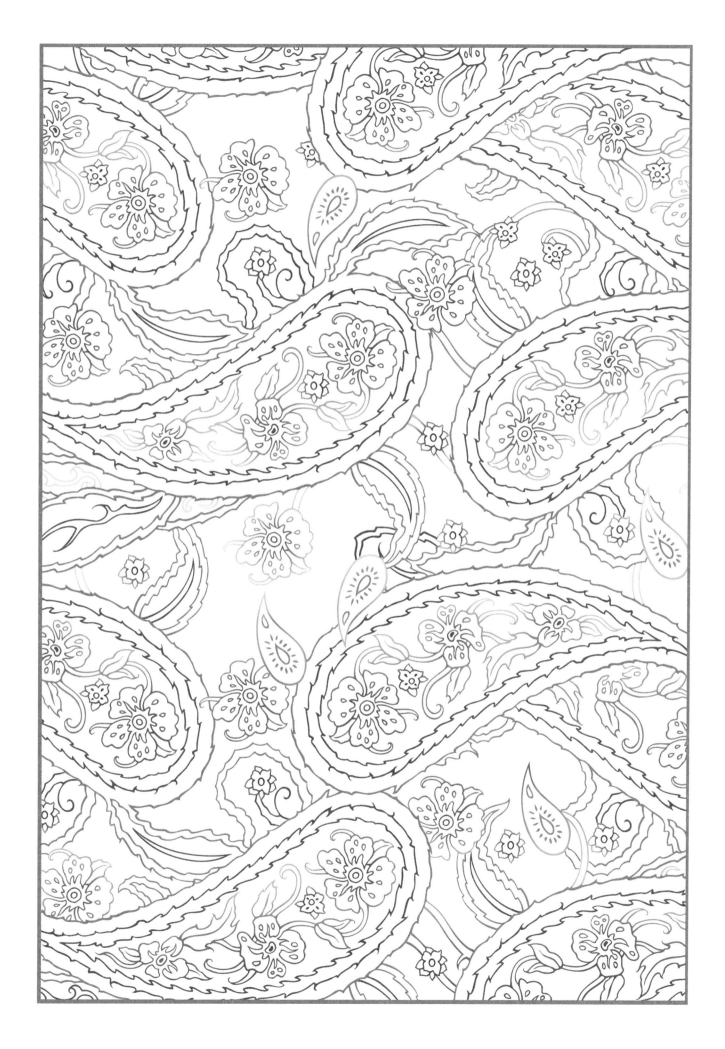

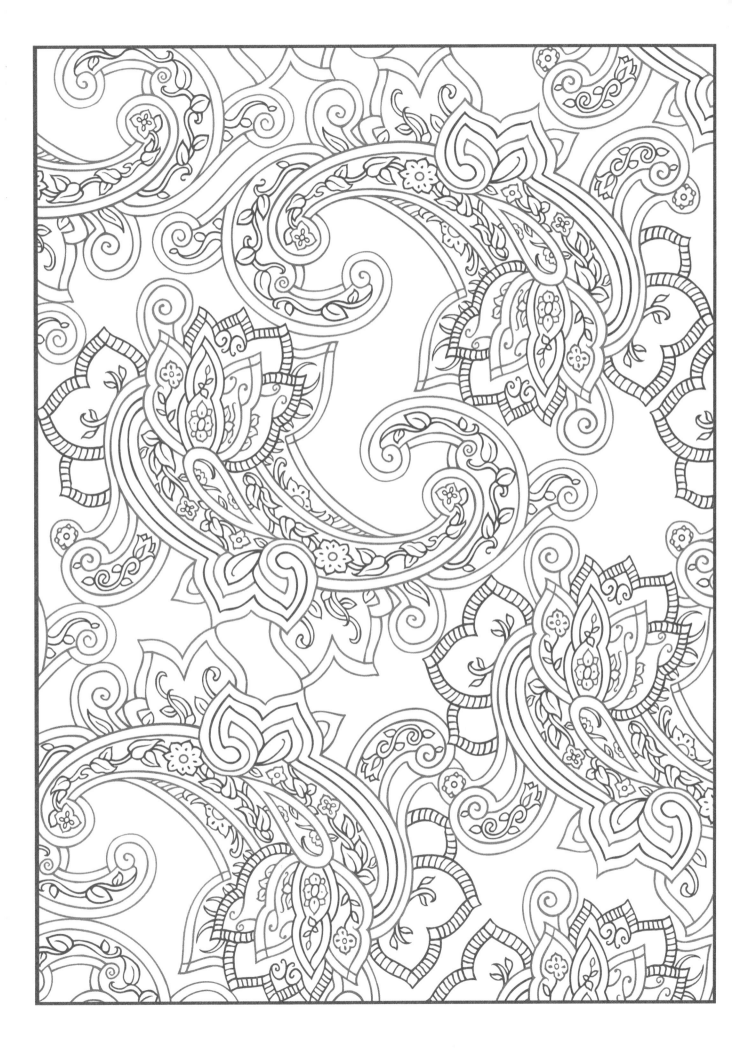

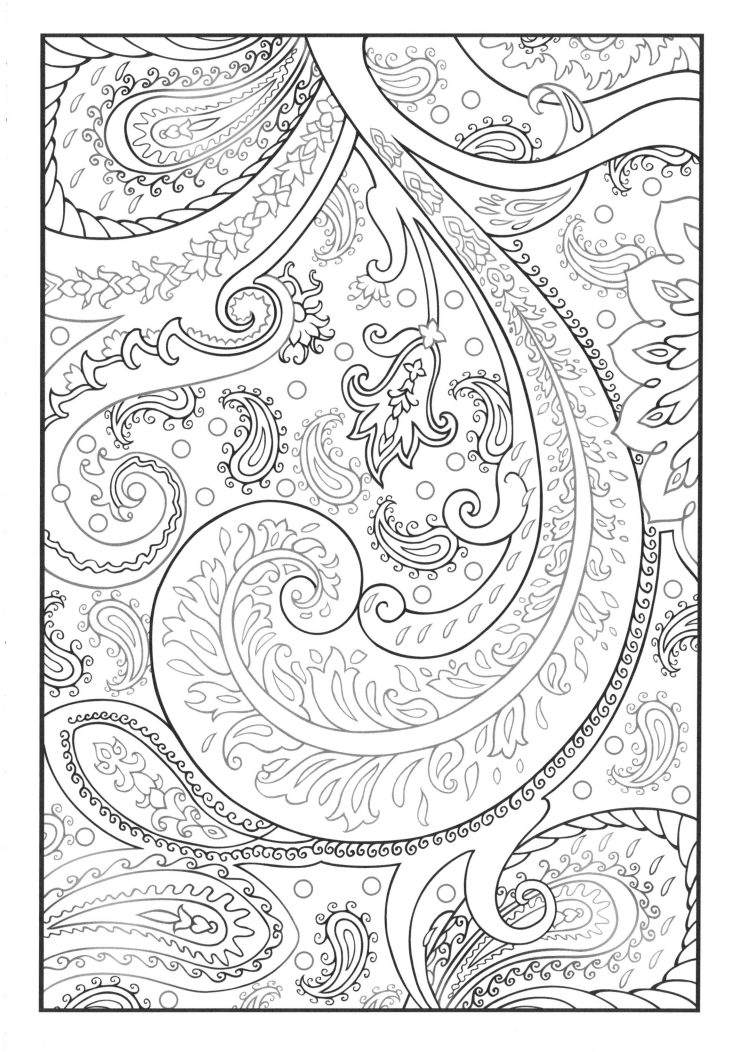

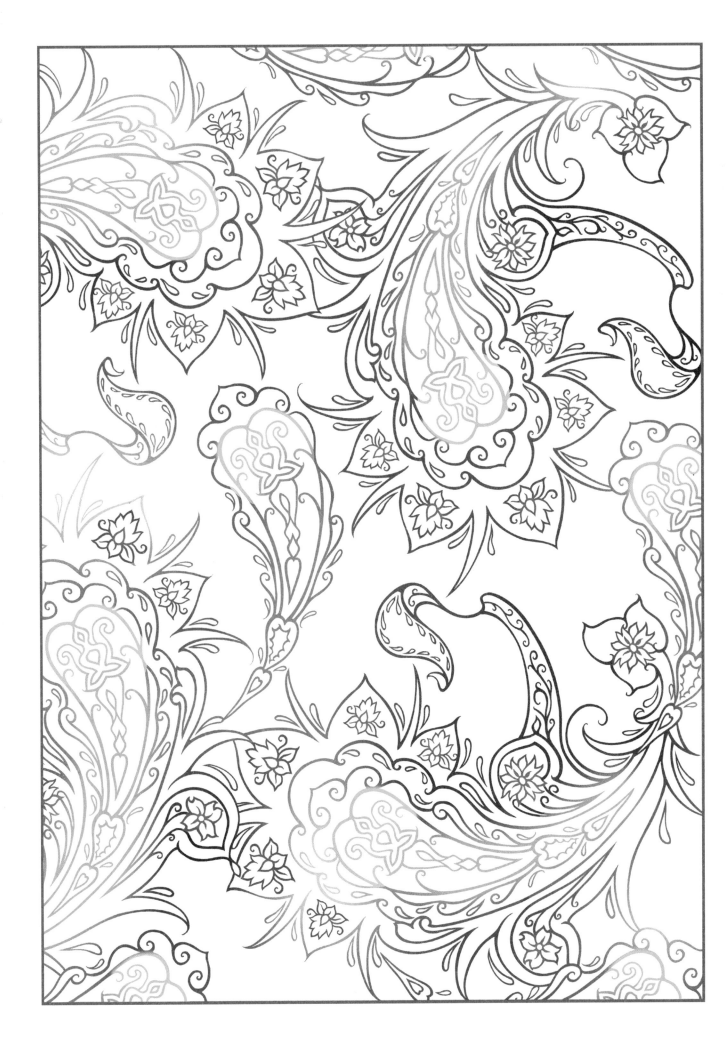

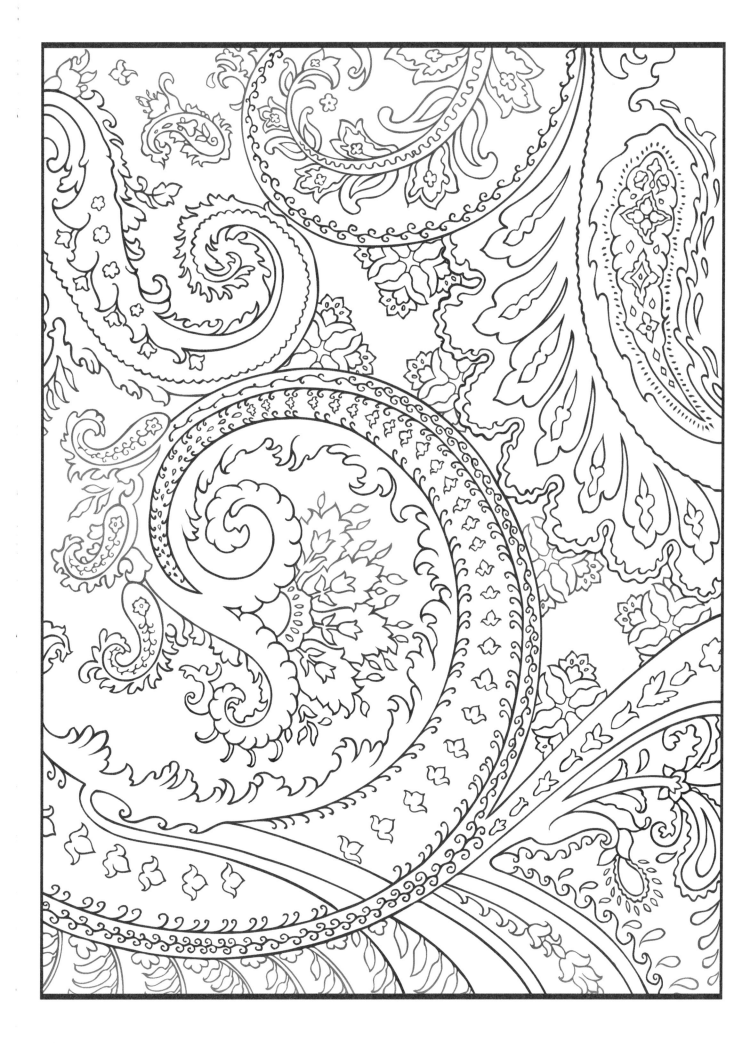

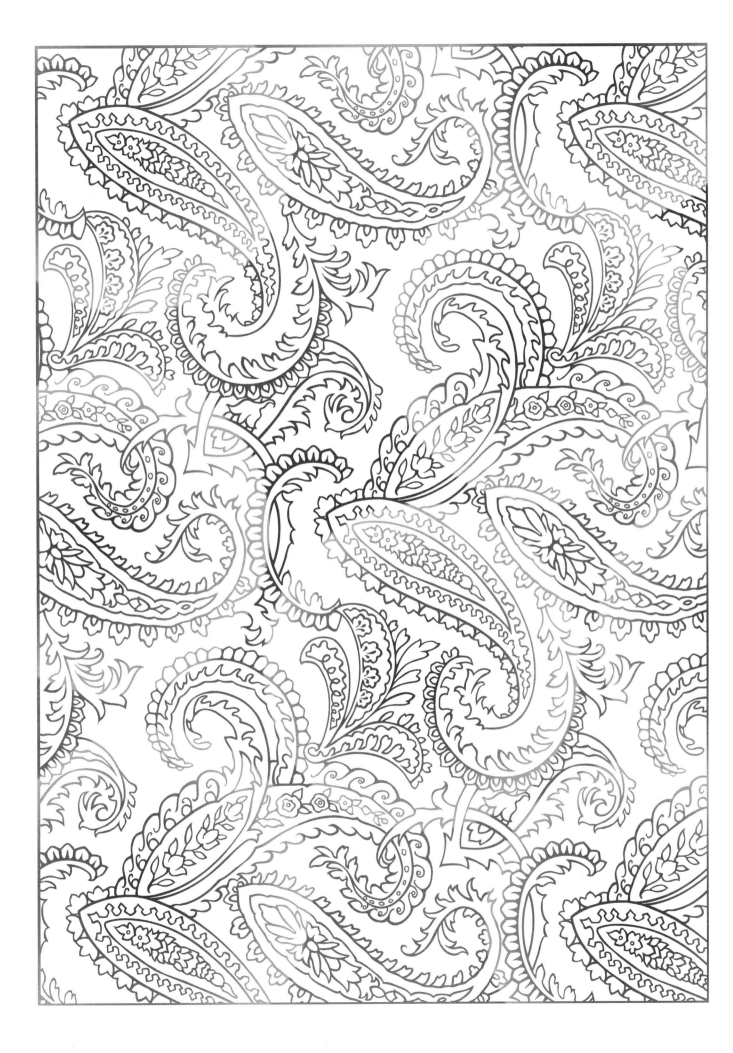

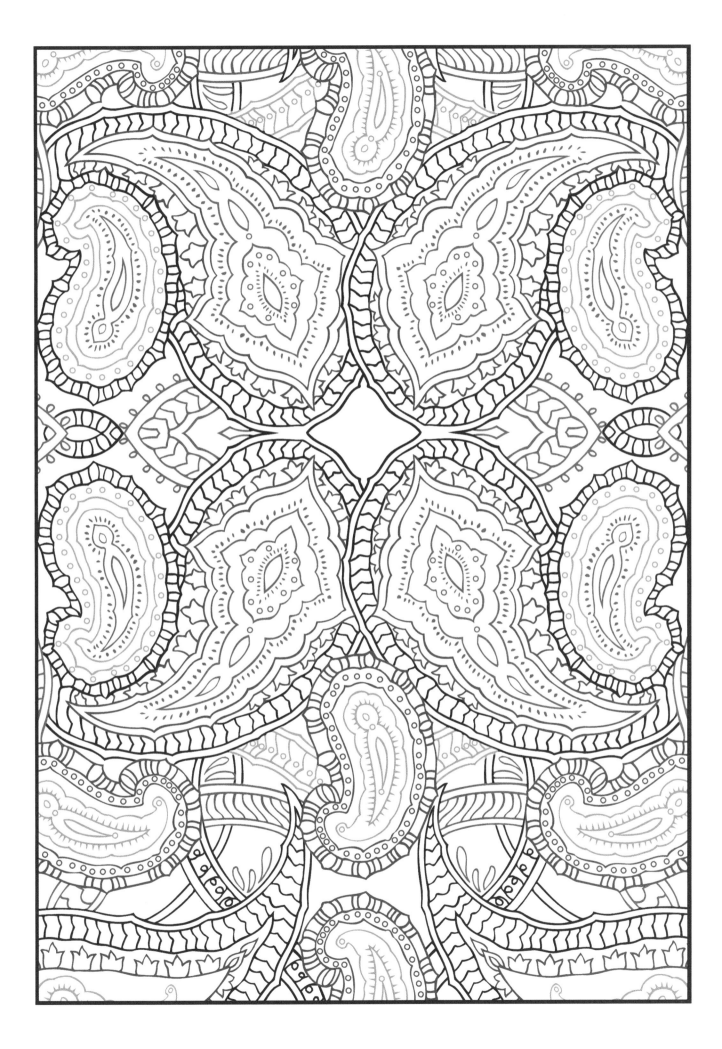

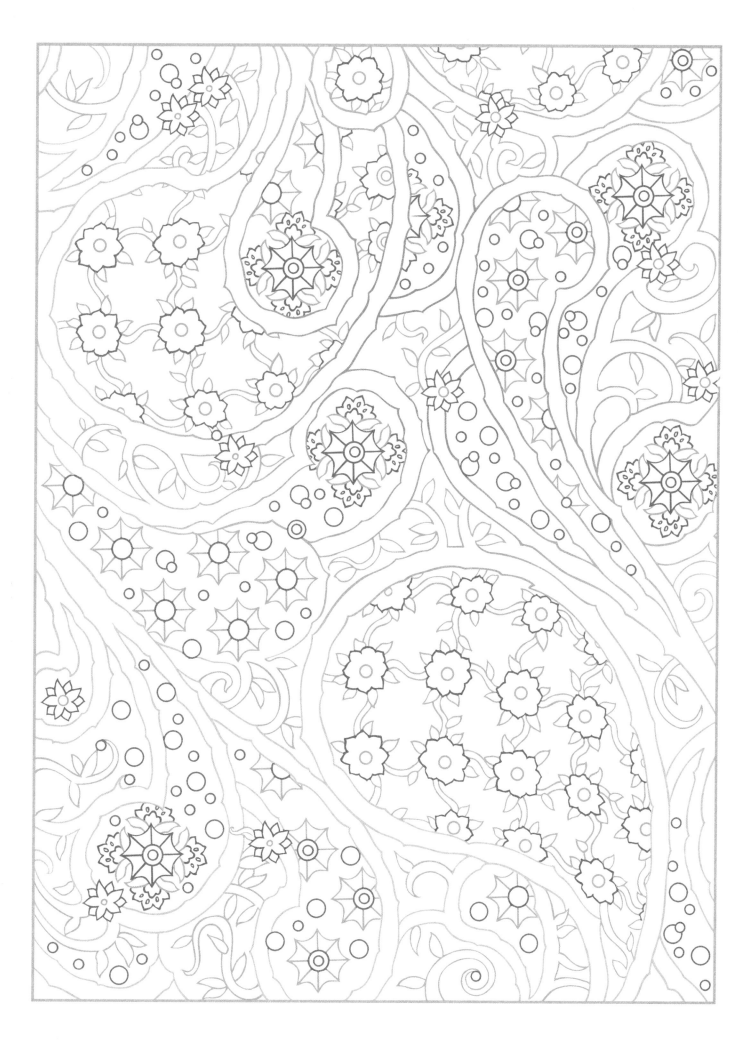

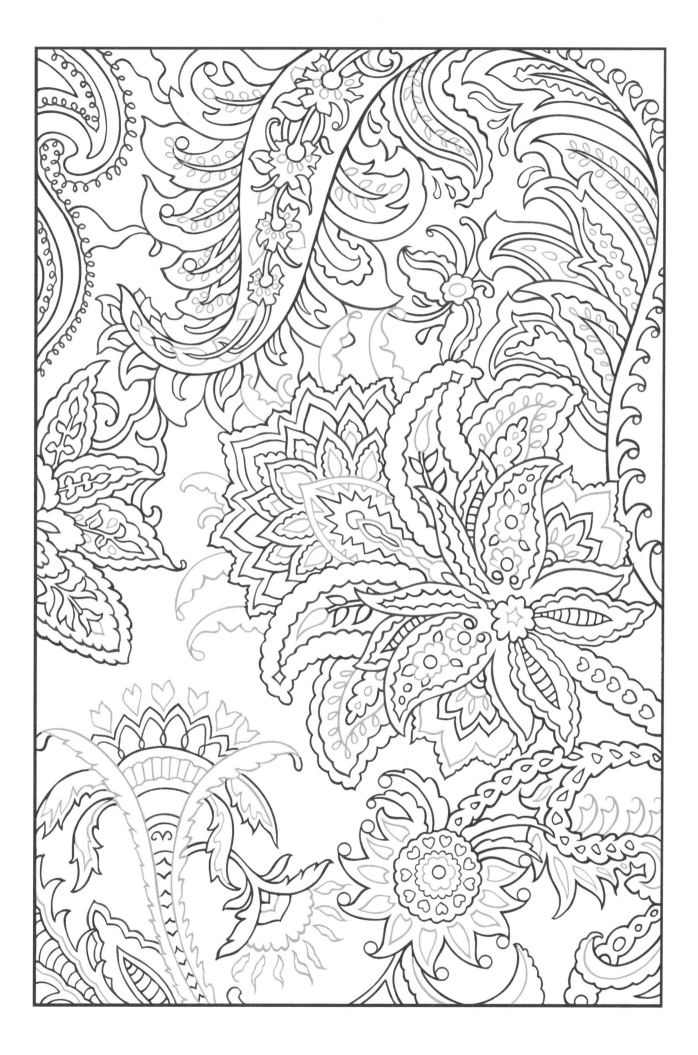

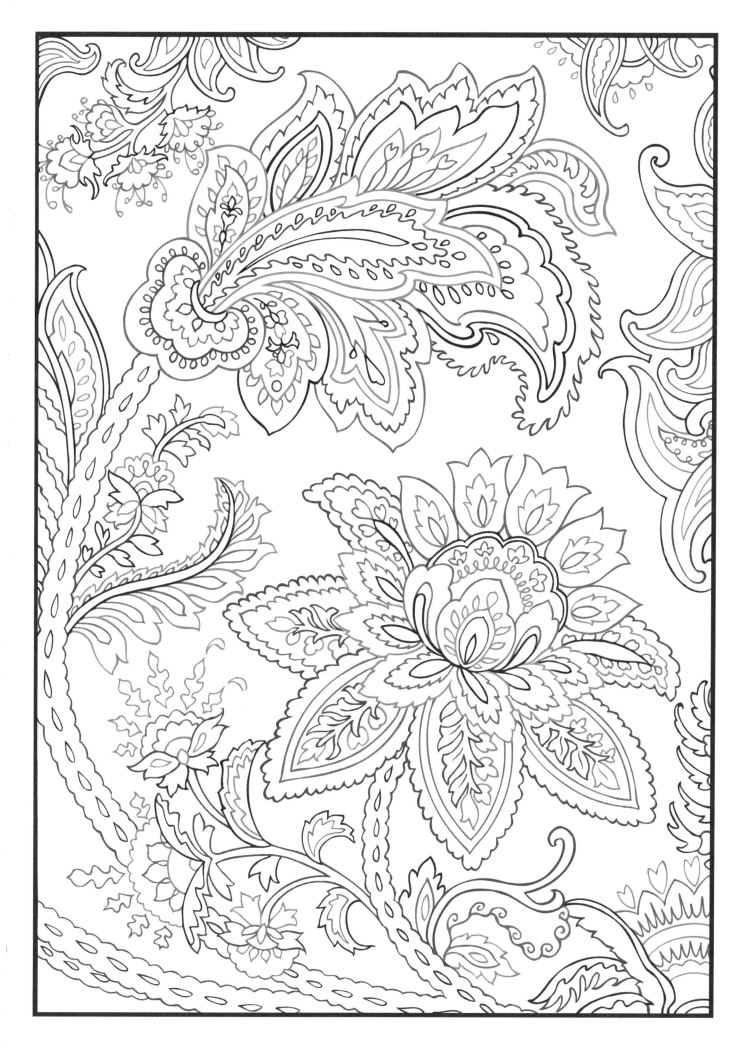

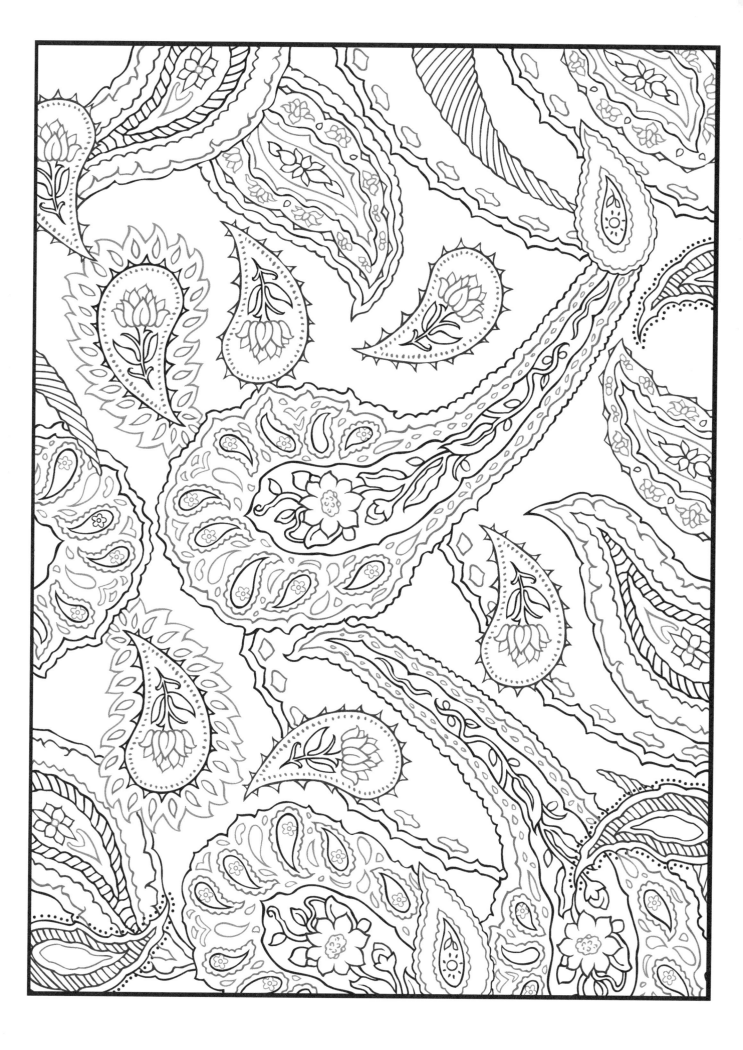

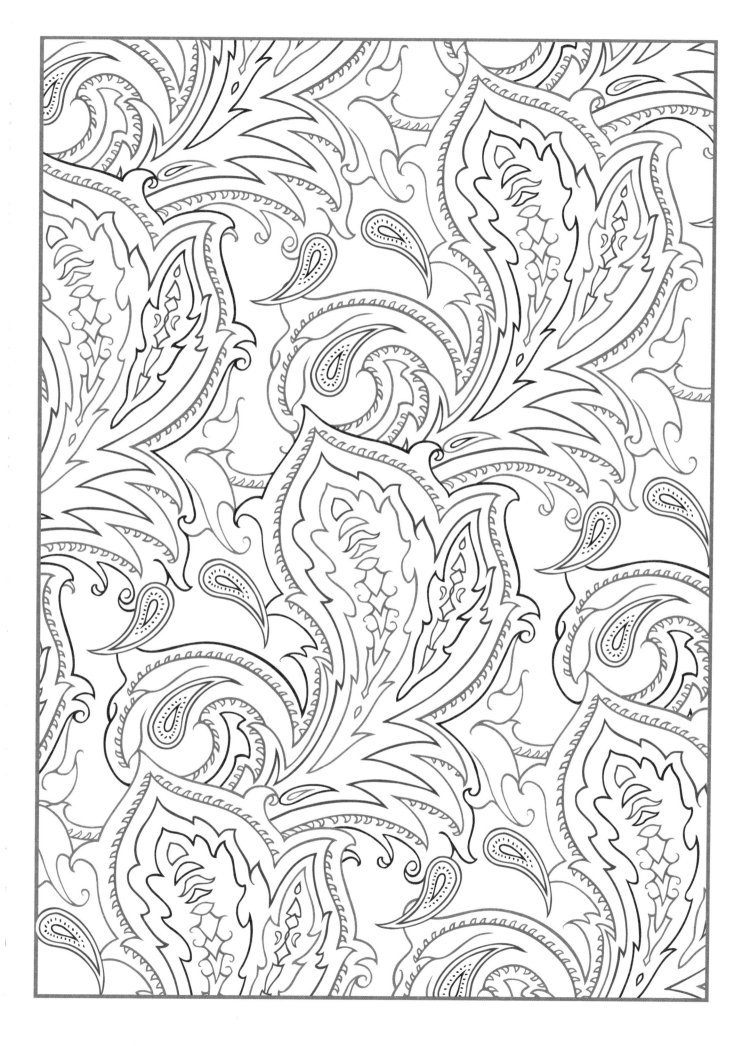